Sheep

Peter Murray

THE CHILD'S WORLD®, INC.

Library of Congress Cataloging-in-Publication Data
Murray, Peter, 1952 Sept. 29–.
Sheep/by Peter Murray.
p.   cm.
Includes index.
Summary: Introduces the physical characteristics,
behavior, life cycle, and different varieties of sheep.
ISBN 1-56766-379-6 (lib. bdg. : alk. paper)
1. Sheep—Juvenile literature. [1. Sheep.] I. Title.
SF375.2.M87   1997
636.3—dc21   97-5953
CIP
AC

Photo Credits

ANIMALS ANIMALS/Peter Weimann: 23
ANIMALS ANIMALS/Victoria McCormick: 29
COMSTOCK/Art Gingert: 2, 10, 13, 16, 30
COMSTOCK/Denver Bryan: 24,26
COMSTOCK/Jack K. Clark: cover, 9, 19
COMSTOCK/Michael Thompson: 6
COMSTOCK/Russ Kinne: 15
William Muñoz: 20

On the cover...

Front cover: This *rambouillet sheep* is waiting to be sheared.
Page 2: This *bighorn ram* is standing on top of a hill.

Table of Contents

Imagine a herd of sheep grazing on green grass. They are covered with a thick coat of soft, curly hair. They look like big balls of dirty cotton! Far away, a shepherd whistles for the sheep to come to him. Soon, the shepherd's dog barks and the herd moves along.

Today, the shepherd wants his sheep to go to the crowding pens, where the sheepshearer waits. It is time for the sheep to get their spring haircuts!

These sheep are gathering in a field to eat and play.

What Do Sheep Look Like?

Sheep hair is called **wool**. The wool from one sheep is called a **fleece**. Sheepshearers use special clippers to cut the fleece close to the sheep's skin. Shearing doesn't hurt the sheep, and in about a year, they grow all of their wool back.

Sheep produce an oil in their skin called **lanolin**. This keeps the sheep's wool soft and dry. After a sheep's fleece is sheared, the lanolin is usually taken out of the wool. Then it can be used for making such things as hand lotion and makeup.

These *rambouillet sheep* are waiting in a pen before they are sheared.

Sheep do not have any top front teeth. Instead, they have a hard, fleshy pad that they bite against with their bottom teeth. When a sheep eats, it bites off pieces of grass and quickly swallows them. Later, when it is relaxing, the sheep will burp up a lump of grass from its stomach into its mouth. This lump of grass is called **cud**. The sheep chews on its cud, grinding it with its hard back teeth

This sheep is eating green grass.

What Are Baby Sheep Like?

Female sheep are called **ewes**. In the late spring, ewes give birth to baby sheep, called **lambs**. Newborn lambs learn to walk only a few minutes after they are born! They grow quickly and are very active. They love to jump and play with each other.

When they are first born, lambs do not eat grass. Instead, they drink a thick milk that their mothers make inside their bodies. After a few weeks, the lambs are old enough to eat grass.

This lamb is standing next to his mother in a field.

What Were Sheep Like Long Ago?

Long ago, all sheep were wild. Then people began capturing the sheep and keeping them for their meat and milk. They also learned how to use the sheep's wool to make warm clothes and blankets.

A wild sheep called the *mouflon* (moo–FLOH) may have been the first relative of today's sheep. Mouflon still roam wild in the countries of Europe and Asia.

These *mouflon sheep* have beautiful curved horns.

Are There Different Kinds of Sheep?

Like many other animals, sheep have been tamed to help people. Different kinds, or **breeds** of sheep have different jobs. Merino sheep are raised for their thick, soft wool. Other types of sheep are raised for their meat or milk. There are more than 800 breeds of sheep in the world today.

This *herdwick sheep* is resting in a field.

Suffolk sheep have dark brown faces and legs. Many farmers like to raise suffolks because they are smart and active. They also can live in areas that do not have a lot of grass. That's because suffolks do not like to stay in one place, like most sheep. Instead, they roam around to find their meals.

Suffolk sheep do not have horns. They have wool that is short and wavy. It is not good wool for making blankets or clothes. Instead, suffolk sheep are raised for their meat and for their milk.

This *suffolk sheep* is much darker than the rambouillet sheep behind it.

Some sheep are able to live in areas with harsh weather. *Navajo sheep* are raised in the dry deserts of Arizona and New Mexico. They have four horns! Their colorful fleece is long, straight and coarse. Wool from Navajo sheep is used to make rugs and blankets.

Navajo sheep like this one have horns on the top and sides of their head.

Some breeds of sheep look different from the sheep you usually see on farms. Fat-tailed and fat-rumped breeds are common in countries such as Asia. These sheep store fat in their rumps or their tails. Most fat-tailed and fat-rumped breeds produce coarse wool that is used to make rugs and carpets.

Hissar sheep like this one store fat in their rump.

What Are Two Kinds of Wild Sheep?

Two types of wild sheep live in North America. *Bighorn sheep* live high in mountain areas. They use their sharp feet, called **hooves**, to climb rocky slopes. The hooves keep the sheep from slipping and falling.

Dall's sheep are similar to the bighorn. They too live high in the mountains. But while bighorns are big and brown, Dall's sheep are mostly white. They are also smaller than bighorns. Both Dall's and bighorns eat the leaves and grasses that grow in the mountains.

Dall's sheep like these can climb high into the rocky hills.

Do All Sheep Have Horns?

Not all sheep grow horns. But some breeds, such as bighorns and Dall's, grow huge, curled horns. In the fall, the male sheep, called **rams**, fight over the ewes. The rams run at each other and bash their horns together. This makes a loud "CRACK!" The noise is so loud, it can be heard from miles away.

These two rams are fighting over some ewes.

Are Sheep in Danger?

Both wild and tamed sheep are sometimes killed by disease or other animals. Coyotes, wolves, and wild dogs are all animals that like to eat sheep. Today, many sheep ranchers use guard dogs to protect their flocks. These dogs are raised with the sheep from the time they are puppies. They live with the sheep and protect them from danger.

This sheep dog is watching over his flock while they are in their pen.

Sheep are one of our oldest tamed animals. For thousands of years, sheep have been raised for their milk and meat. Today, sheep provide us with wool for clothing, blankets, and rugs. The lanolin from their wool is used in hand lotion and makeup. Look around your home and in your closets. Look at the clothing you wear. Look at the fine, curly wool fibers. Can you imagine the sheep it came from?

This *Barbados sheep* is standing in a snowy pen.

Glossary

breed (BREED)
A breed is a kind of animal. There are many different breeds of sheep.

cud (KUD)
Cud is the food that sheep bring back into their mouths after swallowing it.

ewe (YOO)
A ewe is a female sheep.

fleece (FLEES)
A sheep's fleece is its wool coat.

hooves (HOOVZ)
All sheep have sharp feet called hooves. Some sheep have special hooves to help them climb in the mountains.

lamb (LAM)
A lamb is a baby sheep. Lambs like to run and play.

lanolin (LAN–uh–lin)
Lanolin is a special oil that sheep make in their skin. It keeps their fleece soft and dry.

ram (RAM)
A ram is a male sheep. In some breeds, rams fight by bashing their horns together.

wool (WOOL)
Wool is the rough, curly hair that covers a sheep. Wool is used to make clothes, blankets, and rugs.

Index